THE GREAT SOUTHWEST

ACTIVITY BOOK

RISING MOON

The Great Southwest Activity Book
© 2004 by Rising Moon
Illustrations © 2004 by:
Joe Boddy: 34-35
David Brooks: 11, 17, 28-29, 30, 41, 47
Mike Gordon: 3, 4, 9, 32
Peter Grosshauser: 10, 13, 15, 16, 19, 24, 45
Larry Jones: 5, 6, 23, 25, 40
Joe Marciniak: 12, 21, 38, 42, 46, 48
Chris Sabatino: cover, 14, 27, 36

www.risingmoonbooks.com

Composed in the United States of America
Printed in China

Edited by Theresa Howell
Designed by Katie Jennings
Production supervised by Donna Boyd

Printed in Huizhou,Guangdong,PRC,China
November 2019

FIRST IMPRESSION 2004
ISBN 13: 978-0-87358-844-7
ISBN 10: 0-87358-844-4

I'M GOING TO THE SOUTHWEST AND I'M GOING TO PACK....

This is a two-part activity. First things first—you're going to the Southwest and you need to pack. The tricky part is that there's just enough room in the car for you to take one thing for every letter of the alphabet. Take a good hard look at the picture below and mark each item on this page by what letter it starts with.

Next, turn the page and write your list from memory.

DON'T TURN BACK!

I'M GOING TO THE SOUTHWEST AND I'M GOING TO PACK...

Can you remember all of the things you're bringing to the Southwest?
Write a list of what you decided to pack from A to Z.

DON'T TURN BACK!

A _____
B _____
C _____
D _____
E _____
F _____
G _____
H _____
I _____
J _____
K _____
L _____
M _____
N _____
O _____
P _____
Q _____
R _____
S _____
T _____
U _____
V _____
W _____
X _____
Y _____
Z _____

CAR TRIP TIP

While you're riding in the car, you can play this game with your family and friends. Start off with something that begins with the letter **A**. For example, you might say, "*I'm going to the Southwest, and I'm going to bring an armadillo.*" The next person repeats what you said but adds something that starts with the letter **B**. Continue on until you've gone through the whole alphabet. Now that's a good memory!

GO WEST MAZE!

Help this pioneer ride off into the sunset.
Don't get too close to the edge of the winding path!

DESERT ANIMAL SCRAMBLE

These animals are all mixed up. Unscramble the names of the desert animals below.

1. yetoco _____

2. eerd _____

3. nedoarnurr _____

4. vejalani _____

5. ntmiauno olni _____

6. bjacitbkr _____

7. ttsklereaan _____

8. brdhimumgni _____

I SPY A RAINBOW

GREEN   RED   PINK
TURQUOISE   ORANGE   BLACK
BROWN   BLUE   WHITE   PURPLE   YELLOW

The Southwest is a colorful place. Look out the window of your car and see how many things you can find for each of these colors. Keep a list in the spaces below.

Use the colors you've seen outside to help you color this picture. You're the artist!

GAMBEL ON

Who says Ka-KAA-Ka-Ka and wears a fancy topknot? Connect the dots and find out.

FUN THINGS TO DO IN THE SOUTHWEST CROSSWORD PUZZLE

CROSSWORD CLUES

DOWN

2. Pitch your tent and _____.
3. So many curios shops. Let's go _____.
5. Put on your boots and take a _____.
6. In the winter you can go downhill or cross-country _____.
8. You can learn to be a cowboy at a dude _____.
11. Chimichangas, enchiladas, and tacos, oh my! Let's _____ at a Mexican restaurant.
13. You might strike it rich. Pan for _____.

ACROSS

1. Pull out your camera and take lots of _____.
4. Learn about the history, culture, and art of the Southwest by visiting a _____.
7. Spend some time with nature. Visit a National _____.
9. Cast your line and go _____.
10. Giddy up! Spend the day _____-back riding.
12. You're going to get wet on a whitewater _____ trip.

SOUTHWEST PICTURE PUZZLE

Use the pictures below to name some of the amazing plants, animals, and features you might see in the Southwest.

1.  + YAWN = _____

2. 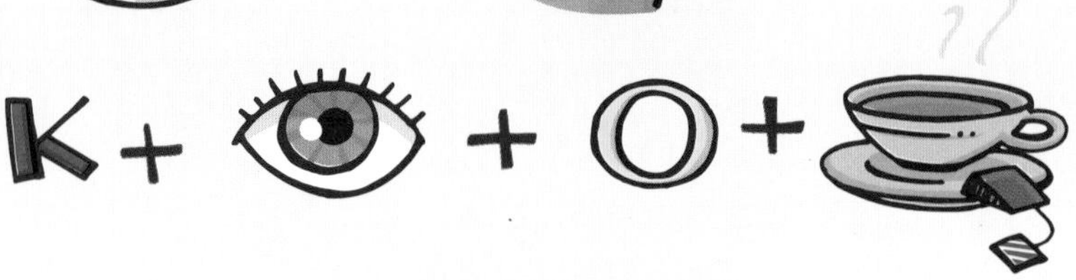 K + + O + = _____

3.  "R" + = _____

4. 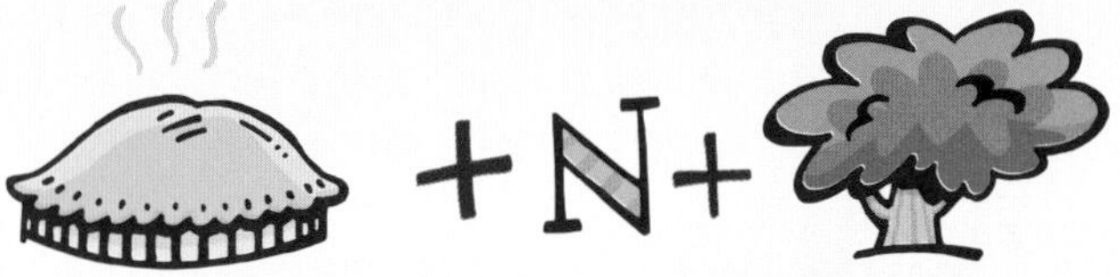 + N + = _____ _____

5.  + = _____

6.  + = _____

7.  + = _____ _____

8.  + + + = _____ _____

PEEK-A-BOO MAZE!

Hidden inside a giant saguaro is this tiny elf owl's nest.
Can you help him find his way back home?

BOO! I FOUND YOU!

Can you find the mining pick, ghost, bucket, hat, jug, tombstone, boot, horseshoe, hair bow, fork, nail, hanger, bottle, wagon wheel, candle, and shovel hidden in this ghost town?

THE WILD DESERT

Bring the color back into the desert!

Number the scenes below to show what happened first, second, and so on during the prairie dogs' train trip to the Southwest.

14

MY SOUTHWEST VACATION

You and a travel buddy can create your own version of your Southwest vacation.
① Don't let your buddy see this page and don't read the story out loud—yet.
② Ask him or her for words to fill in the blanks of the story. Use the words below the blanks as a guide.
③ When you've finished, read the story out loud and find out just how crazy your vacation could actually be.

This summer _____ and I went to _____ . As soon
                  (person's name)   *(place in the Southwest)*

as we got there, I realized that I forgot to pack my _____ .
                                                (a thing)

I brought my _____ by accident. It didn't really matter though
              (a thing)

because we spent _____ weeks _____ and _____ .
                  (number)   *(–ing word)*   *(–ing word)*

One day we saw a _____ from the car window. We started
                    (an animal)

_____ . On our trip we ate _____ almost every day for
(–ing word)   *(a food)*

lunch. It was _____ . I'm going to remember this
                  (describing word)

vacation forever! I took lots and lots of _____ and bought
                                    (things)

a souvenir _____ .
              (a thing)

HAPPY CAMPERS

```
E Q T D S A G B S M O R E S
T V C N S B X R F L O R M Q J L
W C A R W A D M V E T N K I C D
Y U A N H M C Z U A E X L G S A K B
S C B T F C K C L Z P F H M S M F L G
A T G E E B P L V Y I W K H Y P G J F
E F D C E B R A H M I N J E H N F P D L
H Y R X Q N G Q C X I W G N T O K I W K P Q
X G T L P J H I K I N G B O O T S R O D V C
M C M E N P D A W R S H P A R G D Z E T M Y V X
W S Z N F O F L A S H L I G H T O P R Z B Z Z J
B H W T N S N J T N V K O Q X B G M A T C H E S
```

Find the words below hidden in the tent.

WATER

FLASHLIGHT

S'MORES

TENT

SONGS

SLEEPING BAG

MATCHES

MAP

HIKING BOOTS

CANTEEN

BACKPACK

HOT DOG

CAMPFIRE

DOUBLE TAKE!

Look carefully. There are ten differences between these two pictures of a family at the Grand Canyon.
Can you spot them? Circle the differences in the bottom picture.

PETROGLYPH PATH

Help the legendary flute player, Kokopelli, dance his way
through this jumble of ancient rock art.

START

FINISH

IS IT REALLY CALLED THAT?

Can you match each of the town names on the left with a sentence on the right?
No joke—these are all real town names in the Southwest.

1. ___ Strawberry

2. ___ Tortilla Mountains

3. ___ Christmas

4. ___ Chocolate Mountains

5. ___ Carefree

6. ___ Bumblebee

7. ___ Valentine

8. ___ Circle City

9. ___ Cow Springs

10. ___ Tuba City

11. ___ Sunflower

12. ___ Inspiration

13. ___ Tombstone

14. ___ Page

15. ___ Bloody Basin

A.   Watch out! Don't get stung in this town.

B.   Write on this town to make a book.

C.   Poets and artists need what this town already has.

D.   This town is filled with hearts and love.

E.   People in this city don't have any worries.

F.   This town is a part of the band.

G.   There must be a lot of bandages in this spot.

H.   You wouldn't want to visit this town on Halloween.

I.   Are these mountains flat and corny?

J.   There are lots of seeds in this town.

K.   People here must be jolly and merry all year long.

L.   A nice town to make a pie out of.

M.   The farm animals jump really high in this town.

N.   These are the sweetest mountains in Arizona.

O.   There are no squares here!

A BEAUTIFUL NAVAJO RUG

Navajos use many colors when weaving a rug. Color this one in.

CHA-CHING

See if you can find the lollipop, sheep, feather, peach, stamp, arrow, cat, needle, quarter, cow skull, loaf of bread, comb, and paintbrush hidden in the Trading Post.

BEEP!

BEEP!

BEEP!

BEEP!

What bird races around the desert
and can give a rattlesnake a run for its money?
Connect the dots to find out.

1
44 2
43 3
42
41
40 4

38
39 5
37 6 7
36 8

35 11
34 9 12 13
14
33 15
32 16
31
30 29 23 17
22 21 18
20 19
28 24

25
27 26

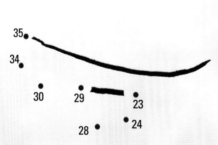

22

COWBOY CODE BREAKER

Use the key to discover a cowboy's #1 rule.

A B C D F G H I J K L M

N O P Q R S T U V W Y

UNDER AND OVER

Can you make it under three of these sandstone arches and over the famous Delicate Arch?

CLUE: Go under one of the arches twice, and avoid any poisonous creatures along the way.

FINISH

START

ARE WE THERE YET?

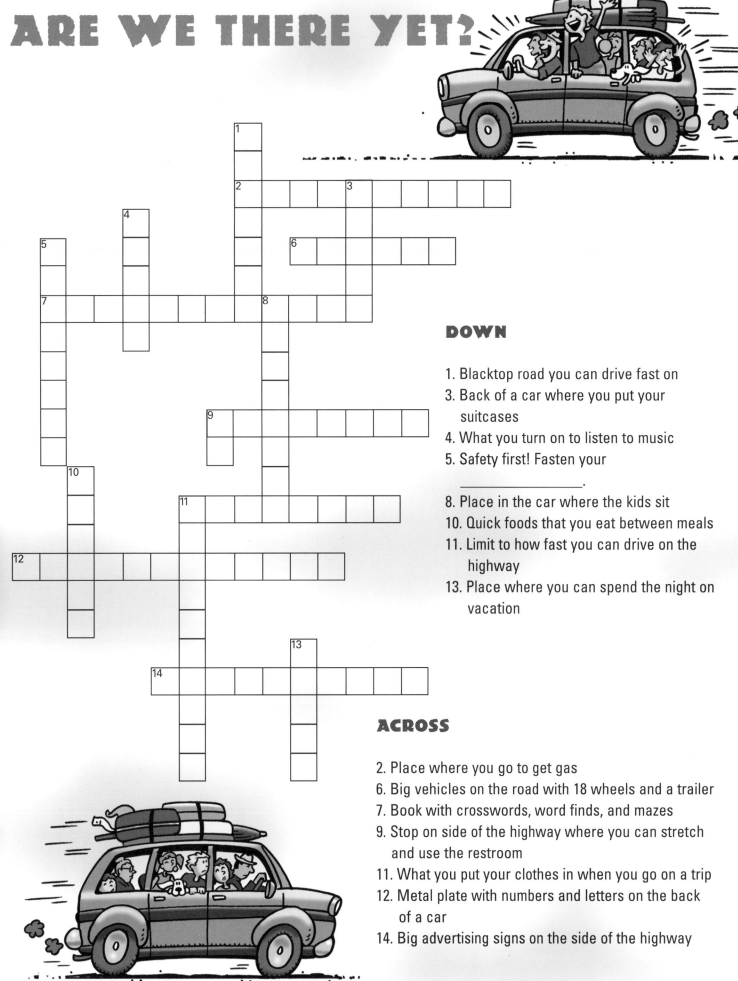

DOWN

1. Blacktop road you can drive fast on
3. Back of a car where you put your suitcases
4. What you turn on to listen to music
5. Safety first! Fasten your

   _____.

8. Place in the car where the kids sit
10. Quick foods that you eat between meals
11. Limit to how fast you can drive on the highway
13. Place where you can spend the night on vacation

ACROSS

2. Place where you go to get gas
6. Big vehicles on the road with 18 wheels and a trailer
7. Book with crosswords, word finds, and mazes
9. Stop on side of the highway where you can stretch and use the restroom
11. What you put your clothes in when you go on a trip
12. Metal plate with numbers and letters on the back of a car
14. Big advertising signs on the side of the highway

FABULOUS DESERT PLANTS WORD FIND

SAGUARO

YUCCA

JOSHUA TREE

SAGE

BARREL

TUMBLEWEED

OCOTILLO

NETTLES

```
                M H U H N N M Q
                I J N I K G O R
                V C V L X A M O
                A T P L O V D F
                R P B G C K O S
                V A M D O X R P
                B L A P T C D C
                J O B O I U A D
                I V C F L E B P              F J H T
S A G E         H E S A L Q H R              J O X U
E A T Z         C R Z Q O A Y I              Y S I M
Y F X A         Q D G V C B M C              N H W B
V U G W                                      C U B L
A S U O     B T X H M W N O L S E N C A Z X K G A H E
F Y D Z     N E T T L E S Y C K A L A O E B L
            G P H F S F G A P T S G N L K D Y U C C A W T M W
            Q W C R E O S O T E W K U K B R P D S O Z I R K E
            H Q J R G E U Z F R F J A O X E J B A R R E L E
                L U E L I R G A H Y P J Q E R D
                I J N I K G O R
                V C V L X A M O
                M H U H N N M Q
                D O V T R P T P
                T L U P S I V R
                G L E Q Y P R S
                T A S I L E U N
                V I G W X M K W
                M J Y A L D O O
                Z B D E V F G E
                V K C J Z E N P
```

CREOSOTE

AGAVE

ORGAN PIPE

PRICKLY PEAR

PALO VERDE

CHOLLA

SOUTHWEST TRAVEL BINGO

Bingo is the name of this game-o. Here's how it works. You and another player each pick a board. Look out your window and mark the picture on your board if you spot it outside. The first person to spot five things in a row—down, across, or diagonally—wins!

ROUND 'EM UP!

HOWDYPARTNER

Help this cowboy round up these stragglin' words. Each word has one spot in the puzzle above. See if you can get them all in line.
HINT: The spaces between the words don't count.

Cattle drive
Stirrup
Campfire
Horseshoe
Brand
Bedroll
Lariat
Buckaroo
Chuck wagon
Guitar
Vaquero

CRAZY FOR KOKOPELLI

Bring this mystical southwestern figure to life with your crayons. Any colors go!

CURIOS

Help these kids pick out a souvenir or two to bring back home. They have exactly 105 tickets to spend in the curios shop. They can't spend a ticket more or a ticket less. Add it up—what goodies can they buy? There are many different combinations. For a bonus, see how many you can find.

SCRATCH PAD

TRAVEL LOG

Use these notepads to record some of the high points (or low points) on your Southwest vacation.

Things I Saw

⭐ My Favorite Day

Things I Did

My Least Favorite Day

HAPPY TRAILS!

Ready. Set. Go! Hike your way from the North Rim
to the South Rim and rest in the Grand Canyon Village.

TOROWEAP OVERLOOK

GRAND CANYON LODGE

Can you find the pot, arrowhead, antler, bone, footprint, fire, petroglyph deer, bow, ear of corn, basket, and handprint in the picture above?

GET YOUR KICKS!
Route 66!

```
L J D B T H C T M B N F S J D P R Y
W T R A V E L E R K V F G O X C A F E Z
B H D G F R G S H F D J K L C U Q C M N
P M A I N S T R E E T Q D T R C H V
J O C W D S G C X V Y H Z I B E
D C T B W O F H B Z C I S O G E
H J V M E L U X Z N T O G P S B S
C Q A S V L V T R Y R L H S X W E X
Y B G M O T H E R R O A D W C F H B Q D
D F J D M K W N L N L P D A W R Q U S R
V Z I K W J T P I K Z X K R Y G T B R C S L
D G F N M Z B H R C I F H I S L Q M G F P K
Q K P E J Q X S Y D C N N R E V H E T J
H L F S R K N H Z M C K K D N X G R X M
G T Y L W K O B R Y Q S R P V I W Y
S M V N A P P L E P I E B L P K T B
T G H O S T R O A D M V N H J M
C G E P Q N W D J H K L
```

KICKS · MOTHER ROAD · SOUVENIR SHOP · OLD HIGHWAY · EXIT · GHOST ROAD · TRAVELER

MAIN STREET · MOTEL · DINER · CURIOS · APPLE PIE · CHEESEBURGER · COLD DRINKS · CAFE

DUST DIABLO

This dust devil is picking up all sorts of things in its path.
Can you pick out a pair of sunglasses, a sock, a lizard, and a baseball?

IT'S A BIG ONE!

What did this lucky angler pull out of the water? Connect the dots to find out.

POSTCARD PONY EXPRESS

Draw a picture of something you've seen on your trip to the Southwest. On the other side of the postcard, write a friend all about it.

¢

PAINTING THE RED ROCKS RED

Brighten up the landscape with your crayons.

This is an important rule to remember
when you're out on the trail.
Use the symbols below to get the message.

A B C D E F G H I J K L M N

O P Q R S T U V W X Y Z

_ _ _ _   _ _ _ _

_ _ _ _ _ _ _ _   .

_ _ _ _ _ _ _ _   _ _ _ _

_ _ _ _ _ _ _ _ _ _   .

MIDNIGHT RIDE

```
        E V B X J G
      G L C F W G M S H V
    D S T A B L E L U F Y O K
  H K R L N F D M S Q B Z C J Z C P
L R O M Z C O L T C W Q S Z R B I D S G
  B H K R C P J Y F K V L E E L G F J A K W O
K L T R Q L D X H O R S E S H O E S M L Y S C O D
T E S P K I E E Z B F T U B D M Z E P G Q A M X Y U T
W N C V J F M D B S G S K Z L Q G N R K H J T R A B W Z S B
H A J T R O T H L B P H R        E P X F V R H R L O
M S P N T L N K P E V U          P D E J K N
X T M W Z X C E C B R
P A Q T S N R E S V
T L V L G T E Y I B
D L F R G M I H C
J I L K S G N L Q
S O S A D D L E
G N F W G X I Y
F B L Z C H N
D F E L K Y Q
N T A I L J
M S P X T P
V A B Z Y H
B R N C Q O
P H M E F O
K H A Y P F
S L R N D
```

Can you find the hidden words?

**BRIDLE ' HORSESHOE ' SADDLE ' MANE ' HOOF
TAIL ' REIN ' STALLION ' MARE ' COLT ' TROT
STABLE ' HAY ' MUZZLE**

HOOOOOWL!

Who howls at the moon? Connect the dots and find out.

11
12
10
9
8
13
14
15
16
7
19
17
20
18
6
21
22
26
27
28
25
5
45
23
29
44
24
4
30
43
31
32
42
41
40
3
33
2
39
37
36
34
38
35
1

OVERBOARD

See if you can find the sunglasses, cooler, soda can, sandal, swim trunks, hot dog, guitar, frying pan, tent, fishing pole, sun hat, suntan lotion, and flashlight in the picture below.

HI-HO-HI-HO

Looks like you struck gold! Help this miner dig up the words in the mine below and put them where they belong. Each word has a special spot in the puzzle. **HINT:** Spaces between words don't count.

P R O S P E C T O R

MULE
COPPER
MILL
DYNAMITE
LANTERN
BUCKET
SILVER
STRIKE
LADDER
DIGGINGS
GOLD
CAMP
SHAFT

HOT FUN IN THE SOUTHWEST

There are no two ways about it—it's a scorcher!
Unscramble the words below and discover 9 different ways to say **HOT**.

HINT: The words are listed above.

1. rubnign _____

2. ingweltsre _____

3. gblioni _____

4. nearsgi _____

5. zlisgniz _____

6. ncrohcisg _____

7. iilfstng _____

8. yunsn _____

9. lestgnirbi _____

JACKELOPE

The Jackelope is a mythical creature of the Southwest. By all accounts he's a combination between a jackrabbit and an antelope—a funny-looking fellow. Who knows what else might be running around out there in the wild!

JACKRABBIT + ANTELOPE=
JACKELOPE

Can you think of names for these other mythical animals?
Use the words below to create names for these other funny-looking fellows.

BEAR ˙ COYOTE ˙ PACK RAT ˙ BOBCAT ˙ JAVELINA ˙ FOX

Now draw some of your own. How about a skunkrunner (skunk+roadrunner), a scorprantula (scorpion+tarantula), or a quailupine (quail+porcupine)?

MY FAVORITE MEMORY

Draw your very own favorite memory of the Southwest. It's like taking a picture.

SOLUTIONS

I'M GOING TO THE SOUTHWEST AND I'M GOING TO PACK...

(pages 3 & 4)

Apple	Jump rope	Sunglasses
Bowl	Knife	Toothbrush
Camera	Lantern	Umbrella
Dog	Map	Volleyball
Envelope	Net	Watch
Fishing pole	Orange	Xylophone
Gloves	Pan	Yo-yo
Hat	Quilt	Zipper
Ice cream cone	Radio	

GO WEST MAZE! (page 5)

DESERT ANIMAL SCRAMBLE

(page 6)

1. coyote
2. deer
3. roadrunner
4. javelina
5. mountain lion
6. jackrabbit
7. rattlesnake
8. hummingbird

GAMBEL ON

(page 8)
Gambel's quail

FUN THINGS TO DO IN THE SOUTHWEST CROSSWORD PUZZLE

(page 9)

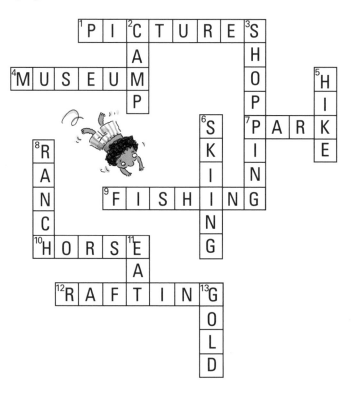

SOLUTIONS

SOUTHWEST PICTURE PUZZLE
(page 10)

1. canyon
2. coyote
3. arches
4. pine tree
5. cowboy
6. rattlesnake
7. ghost town
8. dinosaur bones

PEEK-A-BOO
(page 11)

BOO! I FOUND YOU
(page12)

OUT OF ORDER
(page 14)

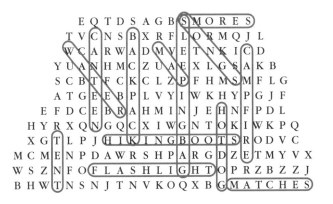

HAPPY CAMPERS
(page 16)

51

SOLUTIONS

DOUBLE TAKE!
(page 17)

PETROGLYPH PATH MAZE
(page 18)

IS IT REALLY CALLED THAT?
(page 19)

1. L
2. I
3. K
4. N
5. E
6. A
7. D
8. O
9. M
10. F
11. J
12. C
13. H
14. B
15. G

CHA-CHING
(page 21)

BEEP! BEEP! BEEP!
(page 22)

roadrunner

COWBOY CODE BREAKER
(page 23)

Don't squat with your spurs on!

SOLUTIONS

UNDER AND OVER
(page 24)

FABULOUS DESERT PLANTS WORD FIND
(page 26)

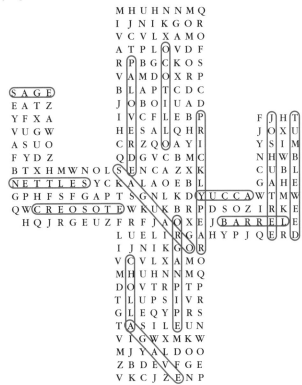

ARE WE THERE YET?
(page 25)

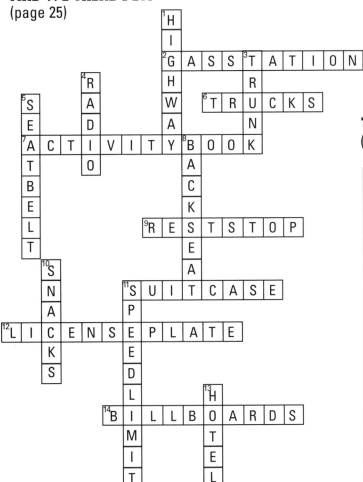

THE DELIRIOUS DESERT
(page 27)

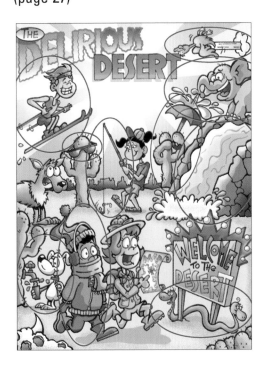

SOLUTIONS

ROUND 'EM UP!
(page 30)

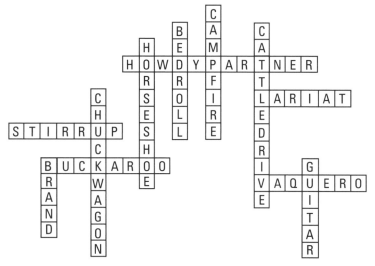

HAPPY TRAILS!
(page 34-35)

CURIOS
(page 32)

With 105 tickets the kids can buy:

- a hat and stuffed animal
- or a necklace and postcard
- or a cactus, activity book, and stuffed animal
- or a paperweight, stuffed animal, and activity book.

HIDDEN ARTIFACTS
(page 36)

SOLUTIONS

GET YOUR KICKS!
(page 37)

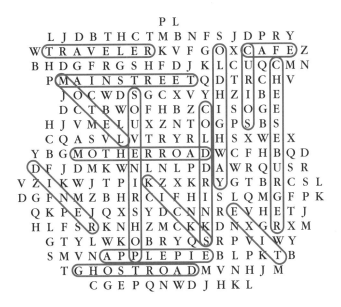

```
                P L
    L J D B T H C T M B N F S J D P R Y
  W T R A V E L E R K V F G O X C A F E Z
    B H D G F R G S H F D J K L C U Q C M N
    P M A I N S T R E E T Q D T R C H V
    J O C W D S G C X V Y H Z I B E
    D C T B W O F H B Z C I S O G E
    H J V M E L U X Z N T O G P S B S
    C Q A S V L V T R Y R L H S X W E X
    Y B G M O T H E R R O A D W C F H B Q D
    D F J D M K W N L N L P D A W R Q U S R
    V Z I K W J T P I K Z X K R Y G T B R C S L
    D G F N M Z B H R C I F H I S L Q M G F P K
    Q K P E J Q X S Y D C N N R E V H E T J
    H L F S R K N H Z M C K K D N X G R X M
    G T Y L W K O B R Y Q S R P V I W Y
    S M V N A P P L E P I E B L P K T B
    T G H O S T R O A D M V N H J M
        C G E P Q N W D J H K L
```

DUST DIABLO
(page 38)

IT'S A BIG ONE!
(page 39)

fish

LEAVE NO TRACE
(page 42)

Take only pictures. Leave only footprints.

MIDNIGHT RIDE
(page 43)

```
                    E V B X J G
                  G L C F W G M S H V
                D S T A B L E L U F Y O K
              H K R L N F D M S Q B Z C J Z C P
            L R O M Z C O L T C W Q S Z R B I D S G
            B H K R C P J Y F K V L E E L G F J A K W O
          K L T R Q L D X H O R S E S H O E S M L Y S C O D
        T E S P K I E E Z B F T U B D M Z E P G Q A M X Y U T
    W N C V J F M D B S G S K Z L Q G N R K H J T R A B W Z S B
    H A J T R O T H L B P H R              E P X F V R H R L O
    M S P N T L N K P E V U                    P D E J K N
    X T M W Z X C E C B R
    P A Q T S N R E S V
    T L V L G T E Y I B
    D L F R G M I H C
    J I L K S G N L Q
    S O S A D D L E
    G N F W G X I Y
    F B L Z C H N
    D F E L K Y Q
    N T A I L J
    M S P X T P
    A B Z Y H
    B R N C Q O
    P H M E F O
    K H A Y P F
    S L R N D E
```

SOLUTIONS

HOOOOOWL!
(page 44)

coyote

OVERBOARD
(page 45)

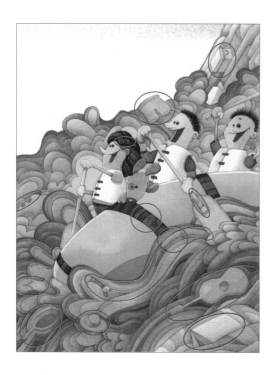

HI-HO-HI-HO
(page 46)

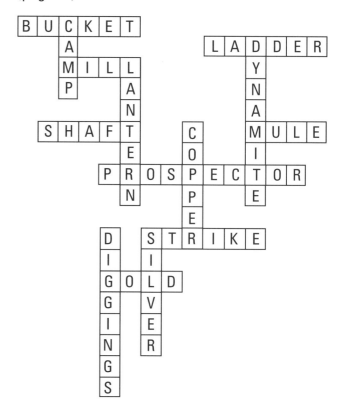

HOT FUN IN THE SOUTHWEST
(page 47)

1. burning
2. sweltering
3. boiling
4. searing
5. sizzling
6. scorching
7. stifling
8. sunny
9. blistering

JACKELOPE
(page 48)

Possible Combinations

Bearyote   Bobrat   Foxalina